Why is the sky blue?

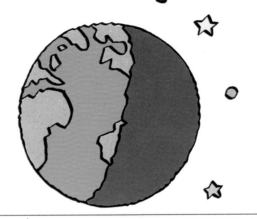

Written by
Alison Niblo and Janet De Saulles

Illustrated by Tony Wells

Watts

LONDON • NEW YORK • SYDNEY

This book tells you about the sky. It explains why it is blue and why it is sometimes other colours too.

We live on a planet called Earth. There is a layer of air around it called the atmosphere. When you look up you can see it high above you. This is what we call the sky.

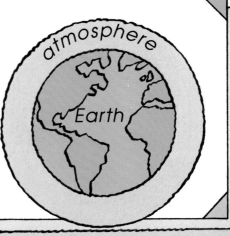

The Sun is far away in space. It is a glowing ball of fire. The Sun shines very brightly. The light it sends out travels through space to Earth.

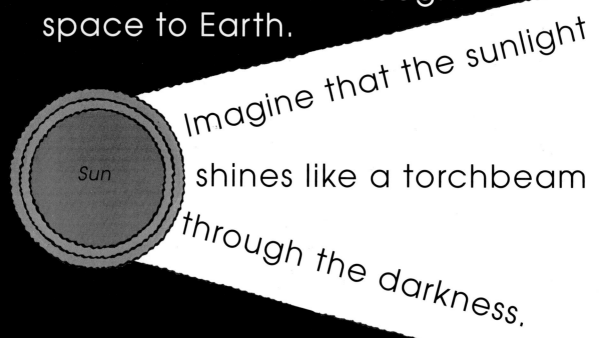

Sun

Imagine that the sunlight shines like a torchbeam through the darkness.

This picture shows sunlight travelling to Earth through black space.

Earth

Stand with your back to the Sun. Your body blocks some of its light, making a shadow on the ground. Can you step on your friend's shadow?

On Earth, the sunlight fills the sky. In summer, the sky is often blue. Sometimes there are fluffy white clouds.

6

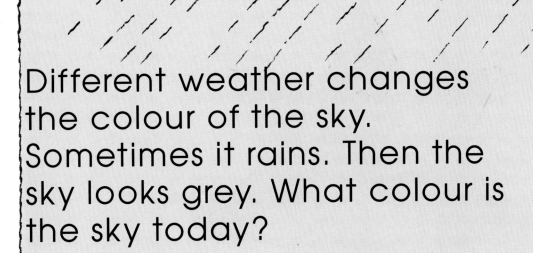

Different weather changes the colour of the sky. Sometimes it rains. Then the sky looks grey. What colour is the sky today?

Try this

Keep a sky colour diary. Every day of the week paint a new page the colours of that day's sky.

What colour do you think sunlight is? It might be a surprise, but it is made of seven different colours!

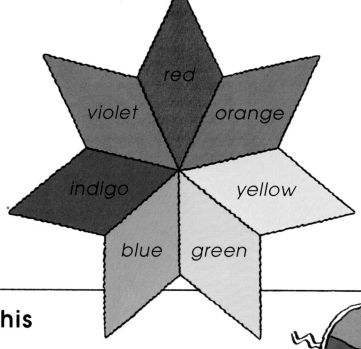

Try this

Divide a card circle into seven sections. Lightly colour them in. Thread string through. Hold the ends and swing the circle round. Pull the string tight so it spins fast. Watch the colours blend together until they look almost white.

Sunlight usually looks clear but when there is a rainbow you can see all the colours. Rainbows form when the Sun shines through raindrops. The raindrops split the light into its seven different colours.

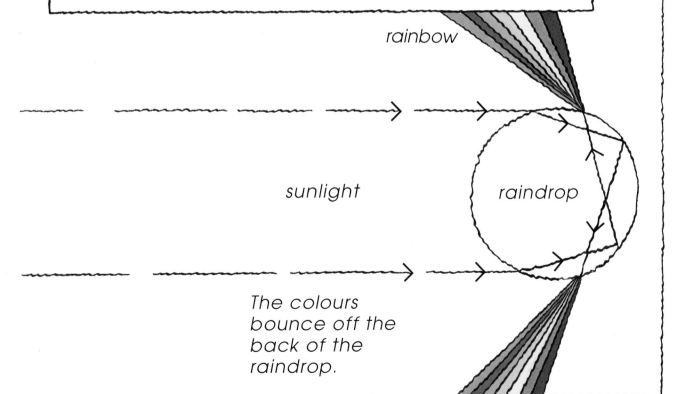

rainbow

sunlight

raindrop

The colours bounce off the back of the raindrop.

The sky is made of air. Air is a mixture of invisible gases that you breathe. Air also has in it tiny specks of dust and drops of water, called particles.

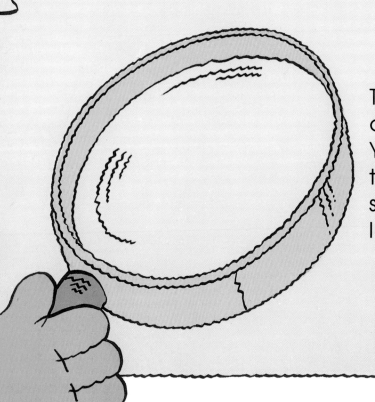

The particles are nearly invisible. You cannot see them, even with a strong magnifying lens.

Try this

On a sunny day, stand near a window and look at the rays of sunlight coming into the room. Can you see dust floating in the sunlight? These are like the tiny particles that fill the sky.

dust

Sun

When sunlight passes through the sky it hits the floating particles and bounces in all directions.

More of the blue light is scattered than any other colour.

That's why the sky looks blue!

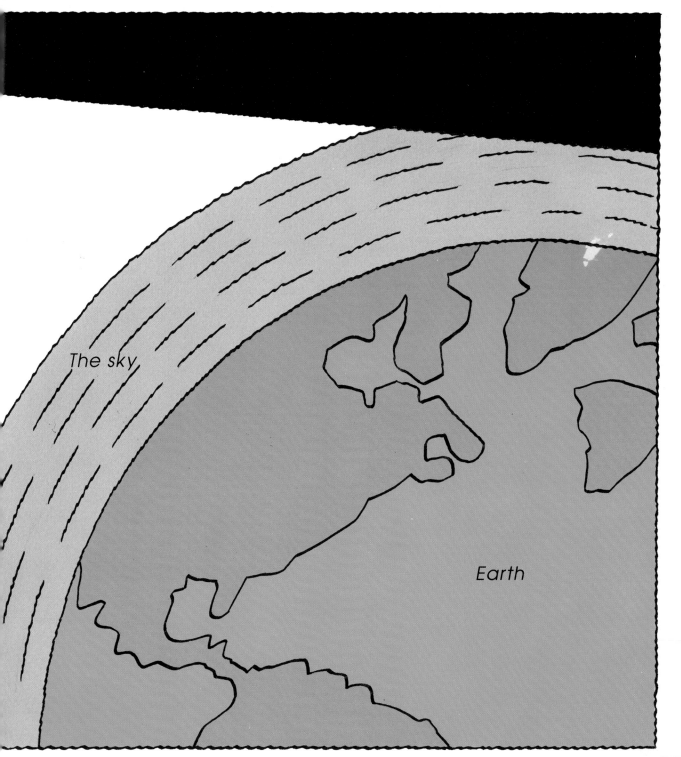

The sky

Earth

Sometimes it is misty and clouds cover up the sky. They stop the sunlight shining through.

Make some blindfolds out of dark–coloured
materials and light–coloured materials.
Which material blocks out the light best?
Do dark–coloured materials block out the
light more than light–coloured ones?

white cotton

silky scarf

dark cotton *red material*

The world becomes dark and gloomy.

The Earth turns in space.
When one side of the Earth
is facing away from the Sun it
is night. The sky is black.
Sunlight is filling the sky on the
other side of the planet.

Try this

Find a dark room and shine a torch on to a ball. This is like the Sun shining on the Earth. One side of the ball is light and the other is dark. The Sun makes day and night on the Earth in the same way.

As the day begins or ends, the colour of the sky changes. On a clear day, as the Sun goes down, it might even be orange. This is called a sunset.

The Sun is high in the sky at midday. Its light travels down towards the Earth. At sunset the Sun is low in the sky. You see it through a thicker layer of air that makes the light look orange.

midday

sunset

Earth

Earth

Try this

Make a sunset picture. Cut out coloured tissue paper shapes. Stick them on to a sheet of paper.

Near the North and the South Poles, flashes of colour sometimes light up the sky. These are made by electricity from the Sun.

The Sun's electricity crashes into particles in the air making strange and fantastic colours.

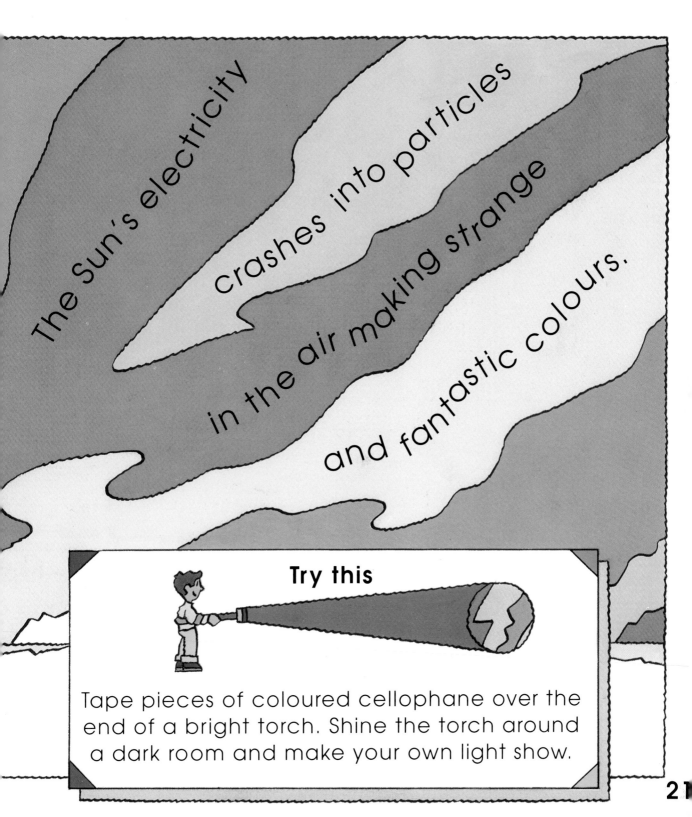

Try this

Tape pieces of coloured cellophane over the end of a bright torch. Shine the torch around a dark room and make your own light show.

Look up at a clear night sky.
The stars you see are other
suns, giving light to millions of
other planets. The stars are too
far away to give much light
to Earth.

The planet Mars is Earth's closest neighbour. Light from the Sun reaches Mars, but the sky is a reddish colour. This is because Mars has no air - only dust particles which make the sky look red.

INDEX

Produced by Zigzag Publishing Ltd,
5 High Street, Cuckfield, Sussex
RH17 5EN

Consultant: Dr Anne Qualter, Centre for Research in Primary Science and Technology, Liverpool University

Editors: Janet De Saulles and Hazel Songhurst
Senior Editor: Nicola Wright
Series concept: Tony Potter

Colour separations: Scan Trans , Singapore
Printer: G. Canale & Co, SpA., Italy

First published in 1993 in the UK by Watts Books

BRITISH LIBRARY CATALOGUING IN PUBLICATION DATA
A CIP catalogue record for this book is available from the British Library

Dewey Decimal Classification 551.5

ISBN 0 7496 1177 4
10 9 8 7 6 5 4 3 2 1